LEARNING ABOUT THE EARTH

Oceans

by Emily K. Green

BELLWETHER MEDIA • MINNEAPOLIS, MN

Note to Librarians, Teachers, and Parents:

Blastoff! Readers are carefully developed by literacy experts and combine standards-based content with developmentally appropriate text.

Level 1 provides the most support through repetition of high-frequency words, light text, predictable sentence patterns, and strong visual support.

Level 2 offers early readers a bit more challenge through varied simple sentences, increased text load, and less repetition of high-frequency words.

Level 3 advances early-fluent readers toward fluency through increased text and concept load, less reliance on visuals, longer sentences, and more literary language.

Whichever book is right for your reader, Blastoff! Readers are the perfect books to build confidence and encourage a love of reading that will last a lifetime!

This edition first published in 2007 by Bellwether Media.

No part of this publication may be reproduced in whole or in part without written permission of the publisher. For information regarding permission, write to Bellwether Media Inc., Attention: Permissions Department, Post Office Box 1C, Minnetonka, MN 55345-9998.

Library of Congress Cataloging-in-Publication Data
Green, Emily K., 1966-
  Oceans / by Emily K. Green.
    p. cm. — (Blastoff! readers) (Learning about the earth)
Summary: "Simple text and supportive images introduce beginning readers to the physical characteristics of oceans."
  Includes bibliographical references and index.
  ISBN-10: 1-60014-039-4 (hardcover : alk. paper)
  ISBN-13: 978-1-60014-039-6 (hardcover : alk. paper)
  1. Ocean—Juvenile literature. I. Title. II. Series.

GC21.5.G748 2007
551.46—dc22   2006000606

Text copyright © 2007 by Bellwether Media.
Printed in the United States of America.

Table of Contents

An ocean is a giant body of water. Oceans cover most of the earth.

Ocean water is salty.
It is not good to drink.

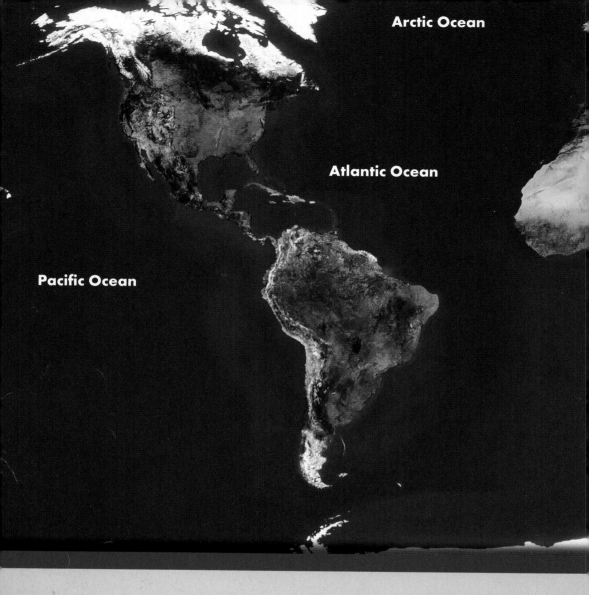

Arctic Ocean

Atlantic Ocean

Pacific Ocean

Earth has five oceans. They are the Pacific Ocean, the Atlantic Ocean, the Indian Ocean, the Southern Ocean, and the Arctic Ocean.

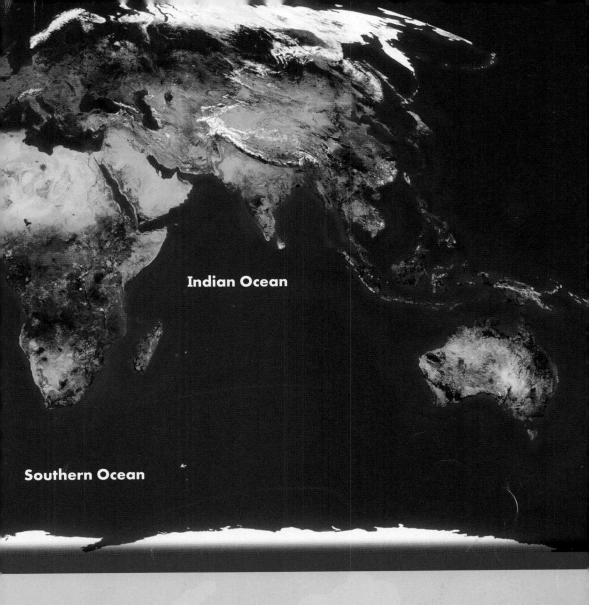

Indian Ocean

Southern Ocean

The five oceans are all connected.

The **coast** is the place where
the water meets the land. Some
coasts are rocky.

Some coasts are flat and covered with sand.

Ocean water is always moving.

Ocean water rises and falls every day. The rise and fall of ocean water is called the **tide**.

Wind blows over the **surface** of the ocean and makes waves. A strong wind makes big waves. Big waves crash against the coast.

A light breeze makes small waves. Small waves ripple on the sand.

Ocean water moves in
the direction of the wind.

The movement of the water is called the **current**. Ships travel with the current.

In some places, the ocean is **shallow**. Sunshine lights up the ocean in shallow places.

In some places, the ocean is very deep. Darkness fills the ocean in deep places. No sunshine reaches there.

17

More kinds of animals live in the ocean than anyone can count. Ocean animals come in many colors, shapes, and sizes.

Thousands of fish live near a **coral reef**. A coral reef is a kind of shell made by tiny ocean animals. Some coral reefs look like colorful gardens under the water.

Some people like to dive under the water to see coral reefs.

Look! There is a beautiful world under the surface of the ocean.

Glossary

coast—the place where the ocean meets the land

coral reef—a structure in the ocean made of the skeletons of coral; coral reefs are only in shallow, sunny parts of the ocean.

current—the movement of water

shallow—water that is not deep

surface—the top

tide—the rise and fall of ocean water

To Learn More

AT THE LIBRARY
Brenner, Barbara. *One Small Place by the Sea.* New York: HarperCollins, 2004.

Karas, G. Brian. *Atlantic.* New York: Putnam, 2002.

Markle, Sandra. *Down, Down, in the Ocean.* New York: Walker & Company, 1999.

Thomas, Meredith. *Rainbows of the Sea.* New York: Mondo, 1998.

Ward, Jennifer. *Somewhere in the Ocean.* Flagstaff, Ariz.: Rising Moon, 2000.

ON THE WEB
Learning more about oceans is as easy as 1, 2, 3.

1. Go to www.factsurfer.com

2. Enter "oceans" into search box.

3. Click the "Surf" button and you will see a list of related web sites.

With factsurfer.com, finding more information is just a click away.

Index

The photographs in this book are reproduced through the courtesy of: George Diebold/Getty Images, front cover; Chad Ehlers/Getty Images, pp. 4-5; Image Makers/Getty Images, pp. 6-7; James Randklev/Getty Images, p. 8; Macduff Everton/Getty Images, p. 9; Jeff Divine/Getty Images, p. 10; Raymond K Gehman/Getty Images, p. 11; Stuart Westmorland/Getty Images, p. 12; Richard Broadwell/Getty Images, p. 13; Pete Seaward/Getty Images, pp. 14-15; Don Hebert/Getty Images, pp. 16-17; Brian Skerry/Getty Images, p. 18; Georgette Douwma/Getty Images, p. 19; A Witte/C Mahaney/Getty Images, pp. 20-21.